ACCOUNTING LIFEP
STARTING AN ACCOUNTIN

CONTENTS

Author: **Daniel L. Ritzman, B.S.**

Editors: **Alan Christopherson, M.S.**
Jennifer L. Davis, B.S.

Alpha Omega Publications®

804 N. 2nd Ave. E., Rock Rapids, IA 51246-1759
© MM by Alpha Omega Publications, Inc.   All rights reserved.
LIFEPAC is a registered trademark of Alpha Omega Publications, Inc.

ACCOUNTING LIFEPAC 2
STARTING AN ACCOUNTING SYSTEM

OVERVIEW

On a regular basis, detailed reports as to the financial condition of a business must be known by its owners and managers. The financial condition of any business can be found on the last line of any accounting equation. However, this is a very informal way of presenting business information. Because of rigid requirements by owners, banking institutions and government agencies, a formal system will be presented in this unit.

OBJECTIVES

When you have completed this LIFEPAC® you will be able to:

1. Define accounting terms associated with starting an accounting system.
2. Identify accounting concepts.
3. Understand the basic accounting equation.
4. Develop a formal balance sheet.
5. Prepare a beginning balance sheet.
6. Create a chart of accounts.
7. Understand the purpose of a general journal.
8. Create a general ledger.
9. Understand the purpose of a general ledger.
10. Record the opening entry.
11. Post the opening entry.

VOCABULARY

Account – a record that summarizes all the characteristics of a single item of the equation.

Account Balance – the computed balance of an account after all debits and credits have been posted.

Account Title – the name given to any account.

Asset – anything of value owned by a business.

Balance Sheet – a form that shows the financial position of a business on a specific date.

Beginning Balance Sheet – a balance sheet prepared on the day the business starts.

Basic Accounting Equation – Assets = Liabilities + Capital.

Book of Original Entry – any journal used in an accounting system.

Book of Secondary Entry – any ledger used in an accounting system.

Capital – the net worth of a business to its owner after all debts are paid.

Chart of Accounts – a list of all accounts used by an entity indicating the identifying number, the account title and classification of each accounting equation item.

Credit – refers to any entry made in the right-hand amount column of a general journal.

Creditor – anyone to whom a business owes money.

Debit – refers to any entry made in the left-hand amount column of a general journal.

Equities – claims against the business assets.

Entry – a transaction recorded in a journal.

General Ledger – contains all the accounts needed to prepare financial statements.

Journal – a business form used for recording accounting information in chronological order.

Journalizing – recording information in chronological order in the journal, using the source document as evidence of the business transaction.

Ledger – a group of accounts.

Liability – any amount of money owed to a creditor.

Liquidity – ease of converting an item to cash.

Opening an Account – writing the account name and number as the heading for the account.

Owner's Equity (Capital) – the financial interest of the owner of a business; determined by subtracting total assets from the total liabilities.

Posting – the process of transferring the information from a journal entry to the ledger accounts.

Source Document – a document that provides the necessary information to make a journal entry.

Transaction – an action that changes the value of the assets, liabilities and capital of a business entity.

SECTION I. DEVELOPING AN ACCOUNTING SYSTEM

As discussed in LIFEPAC 1, a business entity has many items of value, as well as claims against those items. The items are used to produce financial benefits to the business. One such item is an asset. An **asset** is anything of value owned or controlled by a business. Assets are valuable to a business because they are used to purchase other assets or they are used in the daily operation of the business in order to produce revenue.

Claims against assets are called **equities**. A business normally has two claims against its assets: (1) An equity is created when a business owes money. Anyone to whom a business owes money is referred to as a **creditor**. Any amount of money owed to a creditor is called a **liability**. (2) The owner's equity (**capital**) is created when the owner invests in the assets of the business. Since the owner invests in the business, he/she earns the right to decide how the assets are used. The owner's equity is found by applying the accounting equation to analyze changes that occur during daily business operations. By using the accounting equation, the owner's equity is determined by subtracting the total assets from total liabilities.

In order to explain the relationship between assets, liabilities and capital, the **basic accounting equation** was created. This equation (Assets = Liabilities + Capital) must always be in balance. That is, the totals on the left side must always equal the totals on the right side. These totals are changed by normal, day-to-day business transactions. A **transaction** changes the value of the assets, liabilities and capital of a business entity.

Every day a business will engage in hundreds of business transactions involving all types of assets, liabilities and equity. Most of these activities occur several times a day during normal business hours. Since these transactions are repetitive, they can be grouped in categories with common characteristics.

A record that summarizes all the characteristics of a single item of the accounting equation is called an **account**. The name given to any account is called an **account title**. As an example, a business will have many transactions involving the receipt or payment of cash. The bookkeeper or accountant will set up an account entitled "Cash." By doing this, the accountant, bookkeeper or owner need only look in this account to answer any questions concerning cash transactions that might arise during an accounting period. The **account balance** is determined by summarizing the changes to any single account, comparing increases and decreases and bringing forward the total debit balance or credit balance.

In LIFEPAC 1, you balanced the accounting equation every time a transaction was recorded. Preparing a new equation (A = L + C) after each transaction is cumbersome and costly, especially considering a business has a great many transactions in an accounting period. Also, information for a specific account such as cash would be lost as successive business transactions were recorded. Any information concerning an account from the accounting equation could be obtained by going back and summarizing each transaction. This would be very time-consuming and the accuracy of the results would be in question.

It is important to design a systematic method of identifying and locating each account used in the accounting equation. A list of all accounts used by an entity indicating the identifying number, the account title and classification of each account is called the **chart of accounts.**

The design of an account numbering system should provide adequate flexibility to permit expansion without having to revise the basic system. Generally, blocks of numbers are assigned to various groups of accounts such as assets, liabilities and capital.

An example of a system designed for a service business might appear as follows:

Assets accounts	110 through 199
Liability accounts	210 through 299
Capital accounts	310 through 399
Revenue accounts	410 through 499
Expense accounts	510 through 599

The first digit indicates the classification of the account and the second or third number indicates the position of that account in the category.

The chart of accounts of any entity is based on two formal reports that must be prepared at the end of every accounting cycle. These two reports are the **balance sheet** and the income statement. The balance sheet will be discussed in the next section. The income statement will be discussed in Accounting LIFEPAC 5.

Creating a Chart of Accounts

1. Use the accounting equation for the basis of the chart of accounts.

Assets	**=**	**Liabilities**	**+**	**Capital**
Left side of an equal sign		*Right side of an equal sign*		

2. Assets are listed in order of **liquidity**. Liquidity is the ease in which asset accounts can be converted to cash.

3. Liabilities are listed in alphabetical order.

4. Owner's equity is listed by investment (Capital), withdrawals (Drawing) and summary accounts.

5. Number the accounts using increments of ten (10). This allows flexibility to add accounts without revising the entire numbering system.

Listed on the following chart are the accounts used by **Pet Groomers**, a business owned by Janet Jones. The accounts are: **Cash**; **Accounts Receivable**; **Supplies**; **Prepaid Insurance**; **Equipment**; **Building**; **Accounts Payable**; **Notes Payable**; **Janet Jones Capital**; and **Janet Jones, Drawing**.

Pet Groomers Chart of Accounts			
ASSETS		**LIABILITIES**	
Cash	110	Accounts Payable	210
Accounts Receivable	120	Notes Payable	220
Supplies	130		
Prepaid Insurance	140	**CAPITAL**	
Equipment	150	Janet Jones, Capital	310
Building	160	Janet Jones, Drawing	320

The first digit of the account number denotes the *division* on the chart of accounts. The second digit denotes the *position* of the account in the division. For example, since we are counting in increments of 10, the number 110 represents the first account in the asset division.

Match each numbered account with the correct description.

1.1 ___e___ Cash (110)

1.2 ___a___ Accounts Receivable (120)

1.3 ___h___ Supplies (130)

1.4 ___d___ Prepaid Insurance (140)

1.5 ___j___ Equipment (150)

1.6 ___i___ Building (160)

1.7 ___g___ Accounts Payable (210)

1.8 ___c___ Notes Payable (220)

1.9 ___b___ Janet Jones, Capital (310)

1.10 ___f___ Janet Jones, Drawing (320)

a. Asset section, second account

b. Capital section, first account

c. Liability section, second account

d. Asset section, fourth account

e. Asset section, first account

f. Capital section, second account

g. Liability section, first account

h. Asset section, third account

i. Asset section, sixth account

j. Asset section, fifth account

5

Using the example on the previous page, create a chart of accounts for The Beauty Chateau.

The **Beauty Chateau** is owned by Mary Murphy. She used the following accounts: **Cash**; **Beauty Supplies**; **Prepaid Insurance**; **Shop Equipment**; **Accounts Payable**; **Notes Payable**; **Sales Tax Payable**; **Mary Murphy, Capital**; and **Mary Murphy, Drawing**.

The Beauty Chateau Chart of Accounts	
Assets	*Liabilities*
a. Cash	f. Accounts Payable
b. Beauty Supplies	g. Notes Payable
c. Prepaid Insurance	h. Sales Tax Payable
d. Shop Equipment	i.
e.	Capital
	j. Mary Murphy, Capital
	k. Mary Murphy, Drawing
	l.

1.11

Points to Remember

1. The numbering system must be flexible.

2. Usually accounts are numbered by 10's.

3. If assets exceed nine accounts, the next asset account number to follow 190 would be 1100. It cannot be numbered 200 because that denotes the liability section.

4. The chart of accounts is designed to fit the accounting equation with assets on the left of the equal sign and liabilities and capital on the right.

Accounting Concepts

Adequate Disclosure: To provide all necessary information on the financial statements of a business so a reader can determine the financial condition of that business.

Basic Accounting Equation: The three elements of any entity are assets, liabilities and capital. The relationship between these elements is expressed by the **basic accounting equation**: Assets = Liabilities + Capital. **Assets** are resources (items owned by a business) that will be used to generate future income. **Liabilities** are debts (something owed) that will transfer assets to others. **Capital** is the net worth of a business to its owner after all debts are paid.

Business Transactions: Every time a business transaction takes place, changes are made within the accounting equation. Every business transaction changes at least two different accounts in the equation.

Going Concern: Every financial report is prepared as if the business will exist forever.

Objective Evidence: Providing a document that supports a business transaction before it is recorded in the accounting system.

Units of Measurement: Applying a value to a business transaction that is represented by a common unit of measurement. In the United States that common value is represented by dollars and cents.

Accounting Practices

Any written item is spelled out completely when space permits. You can abbreviate only if there is not enough space available to write out the entire word.

It is not necessary to use decimal points, commas, a dollar sign or a cent sign when using ruled accounting paper. Columns are usually provided on all accounting paper for the dollars and cents, separating them by lines or shading.

The zeros are written in the cents column for an even amount. Entering the zeros will eliminate confusion at a later date.

Since accounting records are permanent records, all entries should be made in ink. An erasure on an entry or financial report might give the impression that the data has been changed to hide the mishandling of funds.

To correct errors, a single line is drawn through the error and the correct amount or correct title is written above the mistake. This is done to prevent confusion later. All errors should be corrected in a manner that leaves no doubt as to what has occurred.

| Accounts Receivable | | | 6930 | 00 | |
| ~~Accounts Payable~~ | | | ~~6390~~ | ~~00~~ | |

Single lines under a column of numbers are used to indicate addition or subtraction.

Double lines are used to indicate that the work is complete and accurate.

Neatness is extremely important when entering information in accounting records. Many mistakes are made when numbers are not written legibly. It is advisable to use rulers to draw lines and to use non-smear pens.

Review the material in this section in preparation for the Self Test. The Self Test will check your mastery of this particular section. The items missed on this Self Test will indicate specific areas where restudy is needed for mastery.

SELF TEST 1

Fill in the blanks (each answer, 5 points).

1.01　A record that summarizes all the changes of a single item of the accounting equation is called a/an _____ .

1.02　The net worth of a business to its owner after all the debts are paid is called

_____ .

1.03　Claims against assets are called _____ .

1.04　The ease with which assets can be converted to cash is called _____ .

1.05　A list of accounts used by a business indicating the account number, title and classification is called a _____ .

Match the following accounting terms with their definitions (each answer, 5 points).

1.06　_____ anything of value owned by a business

1.07　_____ Assets = Liabilities + Capital

1.08　_____ denotes the division on the chart of accounts

1.09　_____ used to indicate addition or subtraction

1.010　_____ used to indicate that the work is complete and accurate

1.011　_____ denotes the position of the account within the division

1.012　_____ any amount owed

1.013　_____ financial records and reports are completed as if the business will exist forever

1.014　_____ three elements of any entity

1.015　_____ anyone to whom a business owes money

a. first digit in an account number

b. a single line

c. health, wealth, happiness

d. the Going Concern concept

e. assets, liabilities, capital

f. liability

g. assets

h. creditor

i. accounting equation

j. second and third digits in an account number

k. a double line

Answer *true* **or** *false* (each answer, 5 points).

1.016　_____ When using ruled accounting paper, it is not necessary to use zeroes in the cents column when the amounts are even.

1.017　_____ Providing a document that supports every business transaction is called the concept of adequate disclosure.

1.018　_____ Neatness is extremely important when entering information in accounting records.

1.019　_____ A double line is drawn through any error and the correct amount or correct title is written above it.

1.020　_____ Dollar signs are not required when using ruled accounting paper.

| 80 / 100 |

Score _____

✓ Adult Check _____
　　　　　　Initial　　Date

8

SECTION II. FINANCIAL REPORTING

The Balance Sheet

In LIFEPAC 1 you were introduced to the accounting equation as well as the basic concept that its mathematical equality (or balance) must always be maintained. This equation shows the value of the assets, liabilities and capital of a business. These values create a financial position for a business.

The financial statement used to represent these values is called a **balance sheet**. The balance sheet shows the financial position of a business on a specific date. It reports the relationship between business resources (assets), business debts (liabilities) and owner's equity (capital) for that date. Because of this, the balance sheet can be referred to as the "statement of financial position."

The two sides of a balance sheet must always be equal, hence its name. Each transaction changes the equation which, in turn, changes the financial position of that entity. It is important that the two sides equal because one side shows the resources of the business and the other shows who supplied those resources.

A balance sheet can be prepared at any time to report the financial condition of a business. The information required is the net balance of each account at that specific time. These balances can be determined after each transaction. Therefore, a balance sheet could be prepared hourly, daily, or weekly. However, most businesses find it less time consuming and more efficient to prepare this kind of financial report monthly. These financial statements represent the Concept of Adequate Disclosure.

Body of the Balance Sheet. The source of the balance sheet information is the accounting equation (or the balance sheet equation). These equations have three major sections:

1. **Assets** – listed on the left side.
2. **Liabilities** – listed on the right side.
3. **Capital** – also listed on the right side.

The Accounting Equation

ASSETS	LIABILITIES + CAPITAL
(Left side of equation)	(Equities on the right side of the equation)

The Balance Sheet

ASSETS	LIABILITIES
(Left side of equation)	(Right side of the equation)
	CAPITAL
	(Right side of the equation)

By using a "T," it is easy to illustrate both the accounting equation and a balance sheet. The "T" is a visual example of the concept that there is a left and a right side to every accounting equation. It also makes it easier to illustrate the equality of the equation. It is important to note again that the total of the left side (asset section) must equal the total of the equities on the right side (liability section plus the capital section).

Balance Sheet Design. The following balance sheet is for **Pet Groomers**, a business owned by Janet Jones. The balance sheet reflects the financial condition of Janet's business at the close of business on December 31st.

Balance Sheet with One Liability

1	Pet Groomers Balance Sheet December 31, 20—				
2 Assets			**3** Liabilities		
Cash	500	00	Accounts Payable	1000	00
Supplies	200	00			
Equipment	1500	00	**4** Capital		
Prepaid Insurance	400	00	Janet Jones, Capital	1600	00
5 Total Assets	2600	00	Total Liabilities & Capital	**6** 2600	00

1. **Heading:** The centered, three-line heading represents *who* (the business name), *what* (Balance Sheet) and *when* (the date the report is prepared). All business financial reports contain this three-line heading indicating *who*, *what* and *when*.

2. **Asset Section:** This section lists all assets owned by the business. Assets are found on the left side of the accounting equation; therefore, they are listed on the left side of the balance sheet. The account classification "Asset" is centered on the first line of this section. All account titles are listed to the extreme left margin with their respective amounts in the amount column on the left side.

3. **Liability Section:** This section lists all liabilities or debts owed by the business. Liabilities are found on the right side of the accounting equation; therefore, they are listed on the right side of the balance sheet. The account classification "Liabilities" is centered on the first line of this section. All account titles are listed next to the center double line. The amount owed is entered in the amount column on the right side. See the illustration below for the correct format for balance sheets with more than one liability account.

4. **Capital Section:** This section lists the owner's equity in the business. This equity is represented by the Capital account. Capital is found on the right side of the accounting equation; therefore, it is listed on the right side of the balance sheet. The account classification "Capital" is centered on the line beneath Total Liabilities. The owner's name followed by the word "Capital" begins next to the center double line. The amount representing total capital is listed in the amount column.

5. **Total for Asset Section:** A single line is drawn in the amount column above the line representing total assets. The words "Total Assets" are written on the left side of the balance under the Asset section. The total amount is written in the amount column.

6. **Totals for Liabilities and Capital Sections:** A single line is drawn under the amount representing total capital. The words "Total Liabilities and Capital" are written on the right side of the balance sheet on the line under the owner's capital. Notice that Total Assets and Total Liabilities & Capital are directly across from one another, thus presenting a balanced form. Draw two double lines—one under Total Assets and one under Total Liabilities & Capital. These double lines indicate that the totals balance and the form is accurate and complete.

Balance Sheet with Multiple Liabilities

Pet Groomers
Balance Sheet
December 31, 20—

Assets			Liabilities		
Cash	500	00	Accounts Payable 400.00		
Supplies	200	00	Notes Payable 600.00		
Equipment	1500	00	Total Liabilities	1000	00
Prepaid Insurance	400	00			
			Capital		
			Janet Jones, Capital	1600	00
Total Assets	2600	00	Total Liabilities & Capital	2600	00

Preparing a balance sheet. On the next page are the account balances for **Harry's Hobby Shop**. The shop is owned and operated by Harry Henderson. These balances represent the total of all transactions that have occurred for the month of June. Use this information to prepare a balance sheet for **Harry's Hobby Shop**, using the balance sheet for Pet Groomers as an example.

 Prepare a balance sheet for Harry's Hobby Shop.

2.1
a. Complete the three line heading.

b. Prepare the assets section. Assets are on the left side of the balance sheet.

c. Prepare the liabilities section. Liabilities are on the right side of the balance sheet.

d. Prepare the capital section. Capital is on the right side of the balance sheet below the liabilities section. Skip a line between the sections.

e. Determine that the balance sheet is in balance. Using a calculator or scrap paper, add the assets. Then, add the liabilities and capital amounts. Compare the total to prove that they equal each other. In order to complete the balance sheet the left side totals (Assets) must equal the right side totals (Liabilities + Capital).

f. If the figures are in balance, rule a single line across both the left and right amount columns, under the last amount in the longest column. On the next line, write *Total Assets* in the left account title column. In the right column, write *Total Liabilities and Capital*. Rule a double line under both amount columns.

Account Balances for Harry's Hobby Shop

	ASSETS				= LIABILITIES + CAPITAL	
Date	Cash	Supplies	Prepaid Insurance	Equipment	Accounts Payable	Harry Henderson, Capital
June 30	1,550.00	1,725.00	675.00	4,500.00	1,600.00	6,850.00

BALANCE PROOF: 8,450 = 8,450

 Complete a balance sheet for Georgia's Flowers, a flower shop owned and operated by Georgia Jones.

2.2

a. Complete the three-line heading.

b. Prepare the assets section. Assets are on the left side of the balance sheet.

c. Prepare the liabilities section. Liabilities are on the right side of the balance sheet.

d. Prepare the capital section. Capital is on the right side of the balance sheet below the liabilities section.

e. Determine that the balance sheet is in balance. Using a calculator or scrap paper, add the assets. Then, add the liabilities and capital amounts. Compare the totals to prove that they equal each other. In order to complete the balance sheet the left side totals (assets) must equal the right side total (liabilities + capital).

f. If the figures are in balance, rule a single line across both the left and right amount columns, under the last amount in the longest column. On the next line, write *Total Assets* in the left account title column. In the right column, write *Total Liabilities and Capital*. Rule a double line under both amount columns.

Account Balances for Georgia's Flowers

	ASSETS				= LIABILITIES + CAPITAL		
Date	Cash	Supplies	Prepaid Insurance	Equipment	Accounts Payable	Notes Payable	Georgia Jones, Capital
July 31	1,450.00	725.00	1,600.00	5,400.00	1,600.00	1,200.00	6,375.00

BALANCE PROOF: 9,175 = 9,175

The General Journal

It is necessary for the accountant and owner to keep track of business transactions in an orderly fashion. To do this, accounting information must be recorded by date of the business activity. Each transaction must be kept in chronological order.

The business form used for recording accounting information in chronological order is called a **journal**. Each transaction recorded in a journal is called an **entry**. The type of business and the nature of business activities determine the kind of journal the business will need. The accountant has a number of different journals that can be used for a business. For our purposes, they are: (1) a general journal and (2) special journals. Special journals include cash receipts journals and cash payments journals which are used in businesses with a large number of repetitive transactions.

In the preceding LIFEPAC, we discussed the nature of business transactions and the manner in which they are analyzed and classified. We emphasized *why* the transaction affected the accounting equation rather than *how*. We tried to understand the reason for making the entry in a particular manner. We showed the changes caused by the transactions by recording them as they affected each item in the accounting equation. However, this type of entry does not provide the necessary data relating to a particular transaction, nor does it provide a chronological record of these business transactions. The journal will furnish the missing information.

As you think about a journal, think of your assignment book or your diary. The journal is to the accounting system what your assignment book or diary is to you—a daily record of activities. Because it is the first place a written record of business transactions occurs, a journal is referred to as the **book of original entry** for accounting data. The various business transactions are supported by **source documents** such as sales tickets, purchase invoices, checks stubs and so on. On the basis of the source document, the transactions are recorded in chronological order in the journal. Hence, **journalizing** is recording information in chronological order in the journal, using the source document as evidence of the business transaction. After journalizing the daily business transactions, the data is then transferred or posted to the ledger, the **book of secondary entry**.

We will be using the general journal to start our accounting system. A general journal has two amount columns. The left amount column is headed *General Debit*. An entry recorded in the left or debit column is called a **debit**. The right amount column is headed *General Credit*. An entry recorded in the right or credit column is called a **credit**. In regular usage, "debit" means something unfavorable or not good, while "credit" means something to be desired such as "good credit." However, **these meanings do not apply to accounting usage**. "Debit" simply means left side and "credit" means right side. When you debit an account, you are placing an amount on the left side of the account form. When you credit an account you are placing an amount on the right side of the account form.

The "T" formation of the accounting equation and a balance sheet is also seen in the general debit and general credit column of the general journal. The "T" concept is illustrated on the following page.

The Accounting Equation "T"

ASSETS	LIABILITIES + CAPITAL
(Left side of equation)	(Equities on the right side of the equation)

The Balance Sheet "T"

ASSETS	LIABILITIES
(Left side of equation)	(Right side of the equation)
	CAPITAL (Right side of the equation)

Journal Debit and Credit "T"

Date	Account Title and Explanation	Doc No.	Post. Ref.	General Debit	General Credit

JOURNAL					1 Page
Date	Account Title and Explanation	Doc No.	Post. Ref.	General Debit	General Credit
2	3	4	5	6	7

The General Journal:

1. **Page number:** Every journal must have a page number for a reference point.

2. **Date:** Used to record the date of each entry.

3. **Account Title and Explanation:** Used to enter the name of the account debited and the account credited.

4. **Document No.:** Used to enter the number of the source document. Source documents are usually check stubs, sales tickets, purchase invoices or interoffice memos.

5. **Posting Reference:** Cross reference for the location of the transaction, usually the ledger account number to which the transaction was posted.

6. **General Debit Column:** The amount debited.

7. **General Credit Column:** The amount credited.

The General Ledger Account

Any journal contains a daily record of changes in balance sheet items. These changes are the result of ordinary business transactions. Each business activity will change two or more balance sheet items. It is difficult to determine all changes to a single balance sheet item without searching through all entries in a journal. To find the cash balance, for example, you would have to sort through every journal page for entries affecting cash to discover how much the balance has changed or even to determine if there is a balance on hand. Therefore, an accounting form called an **account** was created to sort journal information into separate records for each balance sheet item.

The account is also used to summarize changes in specific balance sheet items. All the accounts from the chart of accounts are assembled in one place called a **ledger**. The ledger that contains all accounts needed to prepare financial statements is called a **general ledger**. There are various methods for keeping the ledger accounts separate in the general ledger. They may be kept on cards, sheets, or in bound book form. Usually a business uses a loose-leaf binder, making it easy to add and remove accounts as needed.

The basic elements of an account form are the two columns used to record debit and credit amounts from a journal. The two amount columns form a "T" as shown.

The Accounting Equation "T"

ASSETS	LIABILITIES + CAPITAL
(Left side of equation)	(Equities on the right side of the equation)

The Balance Sheet "T"

ASSETS	LIABILITIES
(Left side of equation)	(Right side of the equation)
	CAPITAL
	(Right side of the equation)

Journal Debit and Credit "T"

Date	Account Title and Explanation	Doc No.	Post. Ref.	General Debit	General Credit

General Ledger Account "T"

Date	Explanation	Post. Ref.	Debit	Credit	Balance	
					Debit	Credit

18

Account Title: 1					Account No. 2		
Date	Explanation	Post. Ref.	Debit	Credit	Balance		
					Debit	Credit	
3	4	5	6	7	8	9	

The General Ledger Account:

1. **Account Title:** The name of the account: "Cash," for example.

2. **Account Number:** Ledger accounts are numbered and arranged in order in the ledger. Asset accounts usually begin with 100, liability accounts with 200 and capital accounts with 300.

3. **Date:** Record the date transaction occurred here.

4. **Item:** A brief explanation of the transaction goes here.

5. **Posting Reference:** Cross reference for the location of the transaction, usually the page number of the journal from which the transaction was posted.

6. **Debit:** Amount to be recorded as a debit.

7. **Credit:** Amount to be recorded as a credit.

8. **Debit Balance:** Amount of the debit balance of the account (if the account normally has a debit balance).

9. **Credit Balance:** Amount of the credit balance of the account (if the account normally has a credit balance).

The ledger accounts will be discussed in greater detail in Accounting LIFEPAC 4.

Review the material in this section in preparation for the Self Test. This Self Test will check your mastery of this particular section as well as your knowledge of the previous section.

SELF TEST 2

Match the following accounting terms with their definitions. NOTE: some answers may be used more than once (each answer, 2 points).

2.01 _____ the book of original entry

2.02 _____ Assets = Liabilities + Capital

2.03 _____ shows the financial position of a business on a specific date

2.04 _____ left side

2.05 _____ recording information in chronological order in the journal

2.06 _____ right side

2.07 _____ the book of secondary entry

2.08 _____ each transaction that is recorded in a journal

2.09 _____ a form that sorts and summarizes journal information into separate records

2.010 _____ records accounting information in chronological order

a. journalizing

b. debit

c. credit

d. entry

e. the ledger

f. an account

g. Post. Ref.

h. Doc. No.

i. the accounting equation

j. the journal

k. balance sheet

Use the account balances shown below to create a beginning balance sheet for Sweet Susan's Candy Store dated February 1 of the current year (40 points).

Account Balances for **Sweet Susan's Candy Store**

Date	Cash	Supplies	Prepaid Insurance	Equipment	Accounts Payable	Susan Saccharin, Capital
June 30	1,550.00	1,725.00	675.00	4,500.00	1,600.00	6,850.00

2.011

Identify the parts of a journal page by writing the number by the correct description (each answer, 2 points).

Date	Account Title and Explanation	Doc No.	Post. Ref.	General Debit	General Credit
2	**3**	**4**	**5**		

JOURNAL **1** Page

2.012 _____ Used to enter the name of the account debited and the account credited.

2.013 _____ Used to enter the number of the source document.

2.014 _____ Every journal must have one for a reference point.

2.015 _____ Used to record the date of each entry.

2.016 _____ Used as a cross-reference for the ledger accounts for each transaction.

Identify the parts of a ledger account by writing the number by the correct description (each answer, 2 points).

Account Title: _____ **1** _____   Account No. ___ **2** ___

Date	Explanation	Post. Ref.	Debit	Credit	Balance Debit	Balance Credit
3	**4**	**5**				

2.017 _____ Cross-reference for location of transaction, usually the page number of the journal from which the transaction was posted.

2.018 _____ Asset accounts usually begin with 100, liability accounts with 200 and capital accounts with 300.

2.019 _____ When the transaction occurred.

2.020 _____ The name of the account.

2.021 _____ A brief explanation of the transaction.

Score _____

Adult Check _____

Initial   Date

SECTION III. OPENING ENTRIES

Let's Review. Here are some things to remember when preparing a chart of accounts for a business:

1. The chart of accounts is in a "T" form with assets on the left and equities (liabilities and capital) on the right.
2. Asset, liability, and capital accounts each have a distinct numbering system:

    (100) Assets
    (200) Liabilities
    (300) Capital

The chart of accounts for **M & M Bakery** is shown on the next page. The bakery is owned by Margaret Martin. Margaret has listed the following accounts as of June 1 when she started her business. The accounts are: **Cash**; **Accounts Receivable**; **Supplies**; **Prepaid Insurance**; **Equipment**; **Accounts Payable**; **Notes Payable**; **Margaret Martin, Capital**.

M & M Bakery	
Chart of Accounts	
ASSETS		LIABILITIES	
Cash	110	Accounts Payable	210
Accounts Receivable	120	Notes Payable	220
Supplies	130		
Prepaid Insurance	140	CAPITAL	
Equipment	150	Margaret Martin, Capital	310

From the chart of accounts representing the items of the accounting equation, Margaret lists the value of the assets, liabilities and capital. The values are illustrated below:

VALUE OF ITEMS OWNED

Cash	$1,400
Accounts Receivable	600
Supplies	900
Prepaid Insurance	1,000
Equipment	2,600
Total Owned	$6,500

VALUE OF AMOUNTS OWED

Accounts Payable	$1,100
Notes Payable	700
Total Owed	$1,800

These accounts and their amounts are reported on the balance sheet. This balance sheet can be referred to as the **beginning balance sheet** since it is completed the day the business starts.

The balance sheet has three major sections: (1) Assets listed on the left side; (2) Liabilities listed on the right side; and (3) Capital also listed on the right side. Margaret's completed balance sheet is illustrated below.

M & M Bakery
Balance Sheet
June 1, 20—

Assets			Liabilities		
Cash	1400	00	Accounts Payable 1100.00		
Accounts Receivable	600	00	Notes Payable 700.00		
Supplies	900	00	Total Liabilities	1800	00
Prepaid Insurance	1000	00			
Equipment	2600	00	Capital		
			Margaret Martin, Capital	4700	00
Total Assets	6500	00	Total Liabilities & Capital	6500	00

Opening the Ledger

The procedure of writing an account title and account number on the heading of an account form is called **opening the ledger**. A ledger account must be opened for each item listed on the chart of accounts. The general ledger accounts are numbered and arranged in the same order as they appear on the chart of accounts. All of the general ledger accounts listed on the chart of accounts must be opened using the same procedure.

Account Title: *Cash*					Account No. *110*	
Date	Explanation	Post. Ref.	Debit	Credit	Balance Debit	Balance Credit

The Beginning Balance Sheet

The beginning balance sheet is the first information recorded in a new accounting system. This entry is recorded in the general journal. The instructions for this entry have been given on the following interoffice memo from the owner, Margaret Martin. The balance sheet is attached to the memo regarding the opening entry.

Recording the Opening Entry

As stated earlier, every entry needs a source document to support any item that is recorded in any journal. This source document is used as a cross reference for the entry. This supports the accounting concept of Objective Evidence.

The source document to create an opening entry in the journal for M & M Bakery is an interoffice memorandum from the owner instructing the bookkeeper to record the information found on the beginning balance sheet which is attached to the memo.

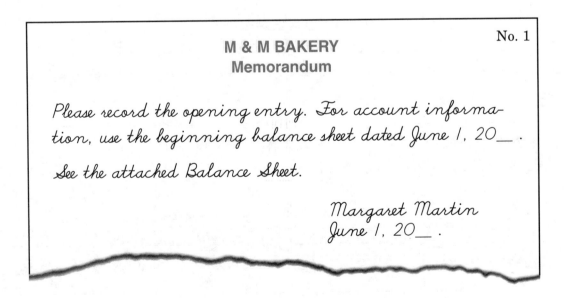

M & M BAKERY
Memorandum

No. 1

Please record the opening entry. For account information, use the beginning balance sheet dated June 1, 20__.

See the attached Balance Sheet.

Margaret Martin
June 1, 20__.

Any supporting accounting data should be attached to the memo, eliminating the need to copy the information to the accounting instructions. Also, under normal circumstances, an entry is not made without the owner's or accountant's signature. After the entry is recorded, the memo is filed by the bookkeeper along with any supporting information.

It is important to keep accounting information organized and all instructions on record as a source of information for future reference. It is easy to remember current transactions, but as months or even years pass by, it will be difficult to reconstruct information without supporting source documents. For the accountant or bookkeeper, an excellent filing system as well as an organized accounting system are very important.

M & M Bakery
Balance Sheet
June 1, 20—

Assets			Liabilities		
Cash	1400	00	Accounts Payable 1100.00		
Accounts Receivable	600	00	Notes Payable 700.00		
Supplies	900	00	Total Liabilities	1800	00
Prepaid Insurance	1000	00			
Equipment	2600	00	Capital		
			Margaret Martin, Capital	4700	00
Total Assets	6500	00	Total Liabilities & Capital	6500	00

Opening Entry Procedure. Let's go through the opening entry a step at a time.

1. **Date and Page Number:** Enter the date of the opening entry in the date column. NOTE: The month is written on the first line only of each ledger page. When a new ledger page is started, the current year is written again as well as the month. Observe the placement of the year in the illustration below. The source document, Margaret Martin's memo, is dated June 1, 20__, which is the first day of business for M & M Bakery. The very first entry in the journal begins on page one.

	JOURNAL					Page /
Date 20—	Account Title and Explanation	Doc No.	Post. Ref.	General Debit		General Credit
June / 1						

2. **Enter Asset Account Titles and Balances:** The name and balance of each asset listed on the balance sheet is recorded first. Each account balance is listed on the left (debit) side.

> **Reminder:** Assets are recorded on the *left* side of the accounting equation and balance sheet. Therefore, asset amounts are entered in the left column of the journal or the debit column.

JOURNAL					Page /		
Date 20—	Account Title and Explanation	Doc No.	Post. Ref.	General Debit		General Credit	
June 1	Cash			1400	00		
	Accounts Receivable			600	00		
	Supplies			900	00		
	Prepaid Insurance			1000	00		
	Equipment			2600	00		

2. **Enter Liability & Capital Account Titles and Balances:** The titles of these accounts are indented about five spaces primarily to indicate that they are credits but also to set them apart visually from the listing of assets. Enter the account balances in the credit column.

> **Reminder:** Liabilities and capital are on the *right* side of the accounting equation and balance sheet. Therefore, liabilities and capital are entered in the right column of the journal or the credit column.

JOURNAL					Page /		
Date 20—	Account Title and Explanation	Doc No.	Post. Ref.	General Debit		General Credit	
June 1	Cash			1400	00		
	Accounts Receivable			600	00		
	Supplies			900	00		
	Prepaid Insurance			1000	00		
	Equipment			2600	00		
	Accounts Payable					1100	00
	Notes Payable					700	00
	M. Martin, Capital	M1				4700	00

(Assets = Liabilities + Capital: 6,500.00   =   6,500.00)

NOTE: "M1" in the Doc. No. column indicates that the interoffice memo No. 1 is the source document for the opening entry.

Accuracy of an Entry. As has been illustrated, the accounting equation and the balance sheet must always be in balance. This means that total assets must equal total liabilities and capital. The same is true of any journal entry. Total debits must always equal total credits. The accuracy is proved by adding the total debit amounts and the total credit amounts which must always be the same.

Posting the Opening Entry

Posting is the process of transferring the information from a journal entry to the ledger account. The posting process sorts all journal entries so that all changes to any accounting equation item are stored in one place.

Posting Procedure. To post the opening entries to the ledger accounts, follow these steps.

Posting the debit parts:

1. Enter the **date of the journal entry** in the date column of the ledger account.
2. Enter a **brief explanation** of the transaction—in this case the opening entry.
3. Enter the **journal page number** in the Post. Ref. column of the account. In the example shown below, *J1* refers to page 1 of the General Journal.
4. Enter the **amount of the debit** in the debit amount column of the ledger account.
5. **Add the amount to any previous debit balance and enter the new balance** in the debit balance column. NOTE: the opening entry balance will be the same as the debit amount since there is no previous balance.
6. **Return to the journal and enter the ledger account number** in the Post. Ref. column. This indicates to which account the amount was posted.

JOURNAL — Page 1

Date 20—	Account Title and Explanation	Doc No.	Post. Ref.	General Debit		General Credit	
June 1	Cash		110	1400	00		
	Accounts Receivable		120	600	00		
	Supplies		130	900	00		
	Prepaid Insurance		140	1000	00		
	Equipment		150	2600	00		
	Accounts Payable		210			1100	00
	Notes Payable		220			700	00
	M. Martin, Capital	M1	310			4700	00

Account Title: Cash   **Account No.** 110

Date 20—	Explanation	Post. Ref.	Debit		Credit		Balance Debit		Balance Credit
June 1	Opening entry	J1	1400	00			1400	00	
1	**2**	**3**	**4**				**5**		

27

Account Title: Accounts Receivable — Account No. 120

Date 20—		Explanation	Post. Ref.	Debit		Credit		Balance Debit		Balance Credit	
June	1	Opening entry	J1	600	00			600	00		

Account Title: Supplies — Account No. 130

Date 20—		Explanation	Post. Ref.	Debit		Credit		Balance Debit		Balance Credit	
June	1	Opening entry	J1	900	00			900	00		

Account Title: Prepaid Insurance — Account No. 140

Date 20—		Explanation	Post. Ref.	Debit		Credit		Balance Debit		Balance Credit	
June	1	Opening entry	J1	1000	00			1000	00		

Account Title: Equipment — Account No. 150

Date 20—		Explanation	Post. Ref.	Debit		Credit		Balance Debit		Balance Credit	
June	1	Opening entry	J1	2600	00			2600	00		

Posting the credit parts:

1. Enter the **date of the journal entry** in the date column of the ledger account.
2. Enter the **journal page number** in the Post. Ref. column of the account.
3. Enter the **amount of the credit** in the credit amount column of the ledger account.
4. **Add the amount to any previous credit balance and enter the new balance** in the credit balance column. NOTE: the opening entry balance will be the same as the credit amount since there is no previous balance.
5. **Return to the journal and enter the ledger account number** in the Post. Ref. column. This indicates to which account the amount was posted.

Account Title: *Accounts Payable*   **Account No.** *210*

Date 20—		Explanation	Post. Ref.	Debit		Credit		Balance			
								Debit		Credit	
June	1	Opening entry	J1			1100	00			1100	00

Account Title: *Notes Payable*   **Account No.** *220*

Date 20—		Explanation	Post. Ref.	Debit		Credit		Balance			
								Debit		Credit	
June	1	Opening entry	J1			700	00			700	00

Account Title: *Margaret Martin, Capital*   **Account No.** *310*

Date 20—		Explanation	Post. Ref.	Debit		Credit		Balance			
								Debit		Credit	
June	1	Opening entry	J1			4700	00			4700	00

Review the material in this section in preparation for the Self Test. This Self Test will check your mastery of this particular section as well as your knowledge of the previous section.

SELF TEST 3

Fill in the blanks (each answer, 3 points).

3.01   The chart of accounts is in a _____ form with assets on the left and liabilities and capital on the right.

3.02   The net worth of a business to its owner after all the debts are paid is called _____ .

3.03   The balance sheet has three major sections: _____ are listed on the left side and _____ and _____ are listed on the right side.

3.04   The first information recorded in a new accounting system is the _____ _____ .

3.05   A _____ is needed for every entry that is recorded in any journal.

3.06   The ease with which assets can be converted to cash is called _____ .

Number the steps for posting the opening entry in the correct order (each answer, 2 points).

3.07   _____   Go to the journal and enter the ledger account number in the Post. Ref. column. This indicates to which account the amount was posted.

3.08   _____   Enter the amount of the debit or credit in the debit or credit amount column of the ledger account.

3.09   _____   Enter the date of the journal entry in the date column of the ledger account.

3.010   _____   Enter the journal page number in the Post. Ref. column of the account.

3.011   _____   Add the amount posted to any previous balance and enter the new balance in the appropriate balance column.

Use the information shown on the balance sheet below to complete the next two activities.

Haines Hardware Emporium
Balance Sheet
April 1, 20—

Assets			Liabilities		
Cash	1000	00	Accounts Payable	1800	00
Accounts Receivable	600	00			
Supplies	2000	00	Capital		
Prepaid Insurance	500	00	Joe Haines, Capital	2300	00
Total Assets	4100	00	Total Liabilities & Capital	4100	00

ACCOUNTING

two

LIFEPAC TEST

100 / 125

Name_____

Date _____

Score _____

LIFEPAC TEST ACCOUNTING 2

PART I

For each item below, circle the letter of the answer that best completes the sentence (each answer, 1 point).

1. The accounting concept that requires that the personal financial records of the owner be kept separate from the business financial records is known as:
   a. going concern
   b. unit of measurement
   c. business entity
   d. adequate disclosure

2. When an accountant prepares financial statements with the intent that a business will exist forever, what accounting concept is he using?
   a. unit of measurement
   b. going concern
   c. business entity
   d. adequate disclosure

3. The accounting formula Assets = Liabilities + Capital is known as the:
   a. accounting equation
   b. business transaction
   c. accounting system
   d. balance sheet

4. When the owner invests in the assets of the business, how does it affect the accounting equation?
   a. assets increase; liabilities increase
   b. assets increase; liabilities decrease
   c. assets decrease; capital increases
   d. assets increase; capital increases

5. For every business transaction, at least two accounts on the accounting equation:
   a. increase
   b. decrease
   c. change
   d. not affected

6. If a transaction decreases one side of the accounting equation, the other side of the equation must:
   a. decrease
   b. increase
   c. not change

7. A business form that lists the account titles used by a business is:
   a. the accounting equation
   b. the balance sheet
   c. the income statement
   d. the chart of accounts

8. If a transaction affects only the accounts on one side of the accounting equation, then:

   a. one account will increase; the other will decrease

   b. both accounts will increase

   c. both accounts will decrease

   d. a transaction can't affect only one side of the equation

9. The financial obligations of a business to another entity are called:

   a. assets   c. liabilities

   b. capital   d. resources

10. What is the purpose of the account title?

    a. indicates the type of transaction recorded in the account

    b. indicates the location in the ledger

    c. provides names of accounts for the bookkeeper to use

    d. indicates its classification

11. What is the purpose of the first digit of an account number?

    a. indicates the type of transaction recorded in the account

    b. indicates the division in the ledger

    c. indicates the classification of the account

    d. used instead of an account title

12. What is the financial function of a balance sheet?

    a. reports the net income of a business on a specific date

    b. reports the financial position of a business on a specific date

    c. reports the current bank balance of the business

    d. reports all of the accounts used by a business

13. What is the purpose of the second digit of an account number?

    a. indicates the transaction type   c. used organized transactions

    b. indicates classification   d. indicates its location within a division of the
                                              ledger

14. The body of a balance sheet contains which of the following account classifications?

    a. assets only   c. assets, liabilities and capital

    b. liabilities only   d. assets and liabilities

15. All financial statements have the same general heading containing:

    a. business name and owner's name

    b. business name and date

    c. business name, name of statement and date of preparation

    d. business name and name of statement

16. The number of accounts used by a business is dependent upon the:
    a. size of the business
    c. the bookkeeper
    b. government regulations
    d. the type of reports to be prepared

17. In preparing a balance sheet, what are the three major sections?
    a. business name, name of statement, date of statement
    b. assets, liabilities and capital
    c. investment, revenues and expenses
    d. capital, assets and liabilities

18. While preparing a business's financial statements, which accounting concept is to be applied?
    a. going concern
    c. business entity
    b. unit of measurement
    d. adequate disclosure

19. A business form used to support or provide supplemental information about a business transaction is called:
    a. an account
    c. a ledger
    b. a source document
    d. a journal

20. Using a single line across an accounting column indicates:
    a. add or subtract the amounts in that column
    b. that the form is complete
    c. start another division of the report
    d. end of the month

21. The first critical step in an accounting system is to:
    a. journalize
    b. post
    c. design an accounting equation
    d. analyze the transaction into its individual parts

22. Any journal used to chronologically record the effects of a transaction on the business accounts is known as the:
    a. general journal
    c. book of secondary entry
    b. general ledger
    d. book of original entry

23. The purpose of a general journal is:
    a. to summarize a transaction
    b. to accumulate information about a transaction
    c. to sort a business transaction into its parts
    d. to provide information to complete a balance sheet

24. The letter used in accounting that helps illustrate the effects of a transaction is:

    a. an X   c. a Y

    b. a T   d. an H

25. The second critical step in an accounting system is to:

    a. journalize

    b. post

    c. design an accounting equation

    d. analyze the transaction into its individual parts

26. What is the procedure for opening an account?

    a. Write the account title and number in the accounting heading.

    b. Only write the account title on the account heading.

    c. Only write the account number on the account heading.

    d. Enter the first amount in the balance column.

27. A business form used to summarize all transactions that affect a single accounting equation item is a/an:

    a. balance sheet   c. ledger

    b. journal   d. account

28. The third critical step in an accounting system is to:

    a. journalize

    b. post

    c. design an accounting equation

    d. analyze the transaction into its individual parts

29. The posting reference column in the journal and ledger are used as a:

    a. numbering system

    b. journal list

    c. cross-reference system to make tracing a transaction easier

    d. method to chronologically record transactions

30. In accounting, account titles, summary information and posting explanations are:

    a. abbreviated whenever possible   c. written in full whenever possible

    b. written above the line   d. written below the line

PART II

Gail Short owns an employment agency called **Job-Find**. The following information has been provided to Gail's accountant:

Assets: **Cash**, $7,500.00; **Office Supplies**, $3,675.00; **Prepaid Insurance**, $1,125.00; **Office Equipment**, $6,675.00

Liabilities: **Accounts Payable**, $3,700; **Notes Payable**, $2,600.00 (NOTE: You must calculate the owner's equity.)

31. Prepare a partial chart of accounts.

32. Prepare a beginning balance sheet. Use January 1 of current year.

33. Record the opening entry; source document is Memo 1.

Date	Account Title and Explanation	Doc No.	Post. Ref.	General Debit		General Credit	
JOURNAL						**Page**	

34. Open the general ledger accounts and post the opening entry.

Account Title: **Account No.**

Date	Explanation	Post. Ref.	Debit	Credit	Balance Debit	Balance Credit

Account Title: **Account No.**

Date	Explanation	Post. Ref.	Debit	Credit	Balance Debit	Balance Credit

Account Title: **Account No.**

Date	Explanation	Post. Ref.	Debit	Credit	Balance Debit	Balance Credit

Account Title:							Account No.	
Date	Explanation	Post. Ref.	Debit	Credit	Balance			
					Debit		Credit	

Account Title:							Account No.	
Date	Explanation	Post. Ref.	Debit	Credit	Balance			
					Debit		Credit	

Account Title:							Account No.	
Date	Explanation	Post. Ref.	Debit	Credit	Balance			
					Debit		Credit	

Account Title:							Account No.	
Date	Explanation	Post. Ref.	Debit	Credit	Balance			
					Debit		Credit	

3.012 Make the opening entry for Haines Hardware Emporium, source document M1 (30 points).

		JOURNAL				Page
Date	Account Title and Explanation	Doc No.	Post. Ref.	General Debit	General Credit	

3.013 Post the opening entry from the general journal to the ledger accounts (42 points).

Account Title: Cash					Account No. 110	
Date	Explanation	Post. Ref.	Debit	Credit	Balance Debit	Credit

Account Title: Accounts Receivable					Account No. 120	
Date	Explanation	Post. Ref.	Debit	Credit	Balance Debit	Credit

Account Title: Supplies					Account No. 130	
Date	Explanation	Post. Ref.	Debit	Credit	Balance Debit	Credit

Account Title: *Prepaid Insurance*   **Account No.** *140*

Date	Explanation	Post. Ref.	Debit	Credit	Balance	
					Debit	Credit

Account Title: *Accounts Payable*   **Account No.** *210*

Date	Explanation	Post. Ref.	Debit	Credit	Balance	
					Debit	Credit

Account Title: *Joe Haines, Capital*   **Account No.** *310*

Date	Explanation	Post. Ref.	Debit	Credit	Balance	
					Debit	Credit

87 / 109

Score _____

Adult Check _____

Initial   Date

SECTION IV. REVIEW & APPLICATION PROBLEMS

Summary

1. Accounting means providing financial information to a number of different users.

2. The three important elements of an entity are assets, liabilities and capital (owner's equity).

3. The basic accounting equation expresses the relationship between assets, liabilities and capital.

4. Assets are the economic resources controlled by a business entity that are used to produce future growth.

5. Liabilities are the debts of a business entity.

6. Owner's equity is the financial interest remaining in the business after all liabilities are paid.

7. A transaction affecting an accounting equation item is summarized in a business form called an account.

8. The account title indicates the type of transaction that must be recorded in that account.

9. A chart of accounts is a listing of the accounts a business is using.

33

10. The balance sheet lists the assets, liabilities and capital of a business entity in order to provide the accountant or owner with information as to the financial position of the entity on a specific date.

11. After completing the balance sheet, journalizing is the next step in the accounting cycle.

12. The journal is known as the book of original entry. It is used to record in chronological order the business transactions of the entity.

13. The general journal is used to record information about a transaction.

14. The general ledger accumulates and summarizes the transactions that affect a particular account.

15. The chart of accounts provides a listing of accounts and their numbers indicating the classification and location of the account in the ledger system.

16. The type of account used is a four-column account which includes a debit and credit entry columns and debit and credit balance columns.

17. After journalizing, posting is the third step in the accounting cycle.

18. Posting is usually done daily, but it can be done anytime, depending on the number of entries accumulated by the business.

19. The ledger account is used to summarize all transactions that affect that particular account.

20. The posting reference column in both the ledger account and the journal provide a means to cross-reference a transaction. This gives the bookkeeper or accountant a method to trace the business transaction if necessary.

Steps for Starting an Accounting System

1. Complete a beginning balance sheet.

2. Complete a source document providing instructions for an opening entry.

3. Record the opening entry from the information provided on the beginning balance sheet. Assets are recorded in the debit column. Liabilities and Capital are recorded in the credit column.

4. Post the opening entry to the general ledger accounts, making sure debit amounts are recorded in the debit column and credit amounts are recorded as credits.

Classify the following accounts either as *assets*, *liabilities* **or** *owner's equity (capital)*. **Place an** *X* **in the appropriate column next to the account title.**

4.1

ACCOUNT TITLE	ASSET	LIABILITY	OWNER'S EQUITY
a. Supplies			
b. Accounts Payable			
c. Cash			
d. Capital			
e. Equipment			
f. Notes Payable			
g. Prepaid Insurance			
h. Sales Tax Payable			
i. Accounts Receivable			
j. Anything of value owned			
k. Any amount owed			
l. Professional library			
m. Withdrawals by owner			
n. Automobile			
o. Owner's equity in anything owned			

Determine the location of the accounts in the accounting equation by indicating on which side the account will be found. Place an *X* **in the appropriate column.**

4.2

ACCOUNT TITLE	LEFT	RIGHT
a. Cash		
b. Notes Payable		
c. Supplies		
d. Accounts Receivable		
e. Sales Tax Payable		
f. Prepaid Insurance		
g. Accounts Payable		
h. Capital		

The purpose of this drill is to classify balance sheet items. The drill also will have you indicate which journal columns are used for each account when recording the opening entry.

 Write the words *asset*, *liability*, or *capital* after the account title in the appropriate balance sheet column. After determining the proper classification, mark an X in the journal column used for that account in the opening entry.

4.3

Item	Balance Sheet		Journal	
	Left	**Right**	**Debit Column**	**Credit Column**
a. Cash				
b. Accounts Payable				
c. Supplies				
d. Notes Payable				
e. Capital				
f. Prepaid Insurance				

Prepare a partial chart of accounts for Johnson's Service Station. The accounts provided by Mr. Johnson are listed below. Be sure to include the appropriate account number.

Cash	Accounts Payable
Accounts Receivable	Notes Payable
Supplies	Mike Johnson, Capital
Prepaid Insurance	
Equipment	

4.4

The elements of a balance sheet below have been assigned a number. For each statement given, identify the element and print the appropriate number in the space provided.

	1					
	2					
	3					
4				5		
	6				7	
				8		
					9	
10					11	

4.5 a. _____ the heading "Assets"

b. _____ the total value of items owned by the business

c. _____ the date of the balance sheet

d. _____ the heading "Liabilities"

e. _____ the name of the business

f. _____ the total equity of the business

g. _____ the total amount of capital

h. _____ the heading "Capital"

i. _____ the value of each amount owed

j. _____ the amount of each asset

k. _____ the name of the business form

Match the numbered parts of the general journal with the correct description.

Date 2	Account Title and Explanation	Doc No.	Post. Ref.	General Debit	General Credit
JOURNAL					Page 1
3	XXXXXXXX 4	5	6	7	
	XXXXXXXX 8				9

4.6 a. _____ the title of the account being debited

b. _____ the reference number of the account to which the item was posted

c. _____ the year of the first entry in the general journal

d. _____ the date the transaction took place

e. _____ the page number of the journal

f. _____ the credit amount for an item being credited

g. _____ the source document for the transaction

h. _____ the dollar value of the account debited

i. _____ the title of the account being credited

Prepare a beginning balance sheet.

Green's Dentistry is owned by John Green. The business's accounting equation is shown below, listing the accounts and their balances.

ASSETS			=	LIABILITIES & CAPITAL	
Cash	Supplies	Equipment		Accounts Payable	John Green, Capital
1,020.00	480.00	9,000.00		500.00	10,000.00

4.7 Prepare a beginning balance sheet for Green's Dentistry. Use January 1 of the current year for the date.

 Prepare a beginning balance sheet.

Downs' Law Office is owned by Joanne Downs. The accounting equation is shown below, listing the accounts and their balances.

ASSETS			=	LIABILITIES & CAPITAL	
Cash	Law Library	Office Equipment		Accounts Payable	Joanne Downs, Capital
1,400.00	2,880.00	6,880.00		1,660.00	9,500.00

4.8 Prepare a beginning balance sheet for Downs' Law Office. Use June 1 of the current year for the date.

 Prepare a beginning balance sheet.

The Bicycle Shop is owned by Harry Smith. The business has the following assets and liabilities:

Assets		Liabilities	
Cash	1,650.00	Account Payable	300.00
Supplies	750.00	Notes Payable	150.00
Prepaid Insurance	980.00	Sales Tax Payable	600.00
Automobile	6,900.00		

4.9   Prepare a beginning balance sheet for The Bicycle Shop. Use August 1 of the current year as the date Harry started business. NOTE: To determine Harry's equity, subtract total liabilities from total assets.

Record an opening entry.

The **Clean-Rite Company** is owned by James King. An interoffice memo and the beginning balance sheet are shown below.

Clean-Rite Company
Memorandum   No. 1

Please record the opening entry. For account information, use the beginning balance sheet (attached) dated January 1, 20__.

James King
January 1, 20__.

Clean-Rite Company
Balance Sheet
January 1, 20–

Assets			Liabilities		
Cash	4105	00	Accounts Payable	350	00
Supplies	2000	00			
Prepaid Insurance	500	00	Capital		
			James King, Capital	6255	00
Total Assets	6605	00	Total Liabilities & Capital	6605	00

4.10   Use the above information to record an opening entry on page 1 of the general journal, dated January 1 of the current year.

	JOURNAL					Page	
Date	Account Title and Explanation	Doc No.	Post. Ref.	General Debit		General Credit	

Record an opening entry.

Henry Harrison is the owner of **Map-It**. Shown below is the beginning balance sheet for his company.

Map-It
Balance Sheet
September 1, 20–

Assets			Liabilities		
Cash	2360	00	Accounts Payable	1550	00
Supplies	2600	00			
Prepaid Insurance	2600	00	Capital		
Equipment	2400	00	Henry Harrison, Capital	8410	00
Total Assets	9960	00	Total Liabilities & Capital	9960	00

4.11   Record the opening entry in the general journal below. Use September 1 of current year with M1 as the source document.

	JOURNAL				Page	
Date	Account Title and Explanation	Doc No.	Post. Ref.	General Debit	General Credit	

Open the general ledger accounts and post the opening entry.

4.12   a. Use the following chart of accounts to open the **Clean-Rite Company** accounts in the general ledger.

b. Post the opening entry that you recorded in the general journal for the **Clean-Rite Company** in **problem 4.10**.

Clean-Rite Company
Chart of Accounts

Assets		Liabilities	
Cash	110	Accounts Payable	210
Supplies	120	**Capital**	
Prepaid Insurance	130	James King, Capital	310

Account Title: **Account No.**

Date	Explanation	Post. Ref.	Debit	Credit	Balance	
					Debit	Credit

Account Title: **Account No.**

Date	Explanation	Post. Ref.	Debit	Credit	Balance	
					Debit	Credit

Account Title: **Account No.**

Date	Explanation	Post. Ref.	Debit	Credit	Balance	
					Debit	Credit

Account Title: **Account No.**

Date	Explanation	Post. Ref.	Debit	Credit	Balance	
					Debit	Credit

Account Title: **Account No.**

Date	Explanation	Post. Ref.	Debit	Credit	Balance	
					Debit	Credit

Open the general ledger accounts and post the opening entry.

Shown below is the chart of accounts for Henry Harrison's business, **Map-It**.

Map-It Chart of Accounts			
Assets		**Liabilities**	
Cash	110	Accounts Payable	210
Supplies	120		
Prepaid Insurance	130	**Capital**	
Equipment	140	James King, Capital	310

4.13   Open the general ledger accounts from the chart of accounts above and post the opening entry that you recorded in the general journal for **Map-It** in **problem 4.11**.

Account Title:					Account No.		
Date	Explanation	Post. Ref.	Debit	Credit	Balance		
					Debit	Credit	

Account Title:						Account No.	
Date	Explanation	Post. Ref.	Debit	Credit	Balance		
					Debit	Credit	

Account Title:						Account No.	
Date	Explanation	Post. Ref.	Debit	Credit	Balance		
					Debit	Credit	

Account Title:						Account No.	
Date	Explanation	Post. Ref.	Debit	Credit	Balance		
					Debit	Credit	

Account Title:						Account No.	
Date	Explanation	Post. Ref.	Debit	Credit	Balance		
					Debit	Credit	

Account Title:						Account No.	
Date	Explanation	Post. Ref.	Debit	Credit	Balance		
					Debit	Credit	

Complete the following activities.

Al Stevenson operates **Al's TV Service**. The information for his beginning balance sheet is given below.

Assets: **Cash**, $1,850.00; **Accounts Receivable**, $690.00; **Office Supplies**, $980.00; **TV Supplies**, $1,150.00; **Equipment**, $5,640.00

Liabilities: **Accounts Payable**, $450.00; **Notes Payable**, $1,230.00; **Sales Tax Payable**, $750.00. (NOTE: Calculate Al's equity by using a variation of the accounting equation: Capital = Assets − Liabilities.)

4.14   Prepare a partial chart of accounts for **Al's TV Service**.

4.15   Prepare the beginning balance sheet for Al's TV Service dated March 1 of the current year.

46

4.16   Record the opening entry on page 1 of the general journal. Source document is M1.

JOURNAL   Page

Date	Account Title and Explanation	Doc No.	Post. Ref.	General Debit		General Credit	

4.17   Open the general ledger from the chart of accounts. Write account names and numbers on each general ledger account, then post the opening entry.

Account Title:					Account No.		
Date	Explanation	Post. Ref.	Debit	Credit	Balance		
					Debit	Credit	

Account Title:					Account No.		
Date	Explanation	Post. Ref.	Debit	Credit	Balance		
					Debit	Credit	

Account Title:					Account No.		
Date	Explanation	Post. Ref.	Debit	Credit	Balance		
					Debit	Credit	

Account Title:					Account No.		
Date	Explanation	Post. Ref.	Debit	Credit	Balance		
					Debit	Credit	

Account Title:					Account No.		
Date	Explanation	Post. Ref.	Debit	Credit	Balance		
					Debit	Credit	

Account Title:					Account No.		
Date	Explanation	Post. Ref.	Debit	Credit	Balance		
					Debit	Credit	

Account Title:					Account No.		
Date	Explanation	Post. Ref.	Debit	Credit	Balance		
					Debit	Credit	

Account Title:					Account No.		
Date	Explanation	Post. Ref.	Debit	Credit	Balance		
					Debit	Credit	

Account Title:					Account No.			
Date	Explanation	Post. Ref.	Debit	Credit	Balance			
					Debit		Credit	

 Complete the following activities.

Barry Holt operates a consulting service known as **Barry Holt, Consultant**. The information for his beginning balance sheet is given below. Subtract total liabilities from the total assets to calculate Mr. Holt's equity (Capital).

Assets:

Cash, $5,600.00;
Accounts Receivable, $8,800.00;
Office Supplies, $500.00;
Prepaid Insurance, $1,200.00;
Land, $18,000.00;
Building, $47,000.00

Liabilities: **Accounts Payable**, $1,400.00; **Mortgage Payable**, $21,700.00; **Notes Payable**, $25,000.00

4.18   Prepare a partial chart of accounts for **Barry Holt, Consultant**.

4.19   Prepare the beginning balance sheet dated October 1 of the current year.

4.20   Record the opening entry on page 1 of the general journal. The source document is M1.

		JOURNAL					Page
Date		Account Title and Explanation	Doc No.	Post. Ref.	General Debit		General Credit

4.21   Open the general ledger from the chart of accounts and post the opening entry.

Account Title:					Account No.	
Date	Explanation	Post. Ref.	Debit	Credit	Balance	
					Debit	Credit

Account Title:					Account No.	
Date	Explanation	Post. Ref.	Debit	Credit	Balance	
					Debit	Credit

Account Title:					Account No.	
Date	Explanation	Post. Ref.	Debit	Credit	Balance	
					Debit	Credit

Account Title:					Account No.	
Date	Explanation	Post. Ref.	Debit	Credit	Balance	
					Debit	Credit

Account Title:					Account No.	
Date	Explanation	Post. Ref.	Debit	Credit	Balance	
					Debit	Credit

Account Title:					Account No.	
Date	Explanation	Post. Ref.	Debit	Credit	Balance	
					Debit	Credit

Account Title:					Account No.	
Date	Explanation	Post. Ref.	Debit	Credit	Balance	
					Debit	Credit

Account Title:					Account No.	
Date	Explanation	Post. Ref.	Debit	Credit	Balance	
					Debit	Credit

Account Title:					Account No.	
Date	Explanation	Post. Ref.	Debit	Credit	Balance	
					Debit	Credit

Account Title:					Account No.	
Date	Explanation	Post. Ref.	Debit	Credit	Balance	
					Debit	Credit

Classify each of the following accounts as either an *asset*, *liability*, **or** *capital* **account.**

	ACCOUNT	CLASSIFICATION
a.	Cash	
b.	Mortgage Payable	
c.	Office Supplies	
d.	Anything of value owned	
e.	Accounts Payable	
f.	Owner's equity	
g.	Prepaid Insurance	
h.	Any amount owed	
i.	Accounts Receivable	

4.22 is to the left of the table, aligned with row a.

Prepare a beginning balance sheet and an opening entry.

George Jones operates **Jones' Trucking**. The information for his beginning balance sheet on January 1 of the current year is below.

Assets: **Cash**, $2,500.00; **Supplies**, $1,150.00; **Prepaid Insurance**, $1,800.00; **Equipment**, $2,400.00

Liabilities: **Accounts Payable**, $1,850.00

4.23   Prepare a beginning balance sheet for Jones' Trucking.

4.24   Record the opening entry on page 1 of the general journal. Source document M1.

Date		Account Title and Explanation	Doc No.	Post. Ref.	General Debit		General Credit	

JOURNAL   Page

OPTIONAL EXERCISES FOR EXTRA CREDIT

 Answer the following questions (each answer, 3 points).

1. What are two fundamental steps in the accounting process that have been studied in this unit?

2. Why is the source document important to a bookkeeper or accountant?

3. What is an account?

4. What is the purpose of the chart of accounts?

5. What is the purpose of the accounting equation?

6. What is the relationship between the amounts on the left side and the right side of the accounting equation?

7. What are the three major sections of a balance sheet?

8. How many balance sheet items are affected by a business transaction?

9. What business form is known as the book of original entry?

10. What are the two steps necessary to open an account?

11. What is the purpose of the posting reference number recorded in the journal after an item has been posted?

12. When recording an entry in a general journal which is written first?

Complete the following activities (100 total points for this exercise).

A month ago, Jane Stone started an interior design business, **Stone's Designs**. Since the business started, she has been keeping the business records as part of her personal financial records. The following information has been provided by Jane to her accountant.

Assets: Cash in Jane's personal account, $650.00; cash in the business account, $1,575.00; office supplies for business, $675.00; homeowner's insurance, $377.00; insurance for the business, $1,125.00; value of personal automobile, $17,500.00; value of the equipment for the business, $12,675.00; value of personal household furnishings, $12,467.00

Liabilities: Balance due for personal automobile, $12,670.00; balance due on the equipment for the business, $9,590.00; personal mortgage on the home, $44,500.00; Visa card balance for clothing purchased, $250.00

13. Separate Jane's personal finances from the business finances, then prepare a chart of accounts (20 points).

14. Use the chart of accounts to prepare a beginning balance sheet. Use September 1 of the current year (20 points).

15. Record the opening entry, source document interoffice memo 1 (20 points).

16. Open the general ledger accounts (20 points).

17. Post the opening entry (20 points).

JOURNAL							Page	
Date	Account Title and Explanation	Doc No.	Post. Ref.	General Debit		General Credit	

Account Title:					Account No.	
Date	Explanation	Post. Ref.	Debit	Credit	Balance	
					Debit	Credit

Account Title:					Account No.	
Date	Explanation	Post. Ref.	Debit	Credit	Balance	
					Debit	Credit

Account Title:					Account No.	
Date	Explanation	Post. Ref.	Debit	Credit	Balance	
					Debit	Credit

Account Title:					Account No.	
Date	Explanation	Post. Ref.	Debit	Credit	Balance	
					Debit	Credit

Account Title:					Account No.	
Date	Explanation	Post. Ref.	Debit	Credit	Balance	
					Debit	Credit

Account Title:					Account No.	
Date	Explanation	Post. Ref.	Debit	Credit	Balance	
					Debit	Credit

		JOURNAL				Page	
Date		Account Title and Explanation	Doc No.	Post. Ref.	General Debit	General Credit	

Account Title:						Account No.	
Date	Explanation	Post. Ref.	Debit	Credit	Balance		
					Debit	Credit	

Account Title:						Account No.	
Date	Explanation	Post. Ref.	Debit	Credit	Balance		
					Debit	Credit	

Account Title:						Account No.	
Date	Explanation	Post. Ref.	Debit	Credit	Balance		
					Debit	Credit	

Account Title:						Account No.	
Date	Explanation	Post. Ref.	Debit	Credit	Balance		
					Debit	Credit	

Account Title:						Account No.	
Date	Explanation	Post. Ref.	Debit	Credit	Balance		
					Debit	Credit	

Account Title:						Account No.	
Date	Explanation	Post. Ref.	Debit	Credit	Balance		
					Debit	Credit	

JOURNAL						Page	
Date	Account Title and Explanation	Doc No.	Post. Ref.	General Debit		General Credit	

Account Title:						Account No.	
Date		Explanation	Post. Ref.	Debit	Credit	Balance	
						Debit	Credit

Account Title:						Account No.	
Date		Explanation	Post. Ref.	Debit	Credit	Balance	
						Debit	Credit

Account Title:						Account No.	
Date		Explanation	Post. Ref.	Debit	Credit	Balance	
						Debit	Credit

Account Title:						Account No.	
Date		Explanation	Post. Ref.	Debit	Credit	Balance	
						Debit	Credit

Account Title:						Account No.	
Date		Explanation	Post. Ref.	Debit	Credit	Balance	
						Debit	Credit

Account Title:						Account No.	
Date		Explanation	Post. Ref.	Debit	Credit	Balance	
						Debit	Credit

Alpha Omega Publications®

804 N. 2nd Ave. E.
Rock Rapids, IA 51246-1759
800-622-3070
www.aop.com

EL9302 – Oct '13 Printing

ISBN 978-0-7403-0185-8

9 780740 301858